INTERNATIONAL STANDARD CERTIFICATION

ISO 10002
Customer Satisfaction
International Standard

For all

Fitness Centers

Jahangir Asadi
Vancouver, BC CANADA

Copyright © 2024 by **ISC** International Standard Certification.

All rights reserved. No part of this publication may be reproduced, distributed or transmitted in any form or by any means, including photocopying, recording, or other electronic or mechanical methods, without the prior written permission of the publisher, except in the case of brief quotations embodied in critical reviews and certain other noncommercial uses permitted by copyright law. For permission requests, write to the publisher, addressed "Attention: Permissions Coordinator," at the address below.

Published by: **ISC** International Standard Certification
Vancouver, BC **CANADA**
Email: Info@ISCASC.com
Web. : www.ISCASC.com

Ordering Information:
Quantity sales. Special discounts are available on quantity purchases by universities, schools, corporations, associations, and others. For details, contact the "Sales Department" at the above mentioned email address.

ISO 10002 for all fitness centers/J.Asadi—1st ed.

Paperback: ISBN: 978-1-77899-010-6

Hardcover: ISBN: 978-1-77899-011-3

Contents

About (ISC) 7
About ISO 10
Definitions 11
What Are the Benefits of Being ISO 10002 Certification? 15
Introduction to Quality Management System (QMS) 21
7 ways to amaze and delight your cutomers 27
Document requirements 29
QM 32
Time frame 34
Control of documents 36
Control of Records 37
Rumi and ISO 41
Bibliography 43
Our latest magazine 45

This book is dedicated to my Professor, Dr.B.Esfandiary

Every possible effort has been made to ensure that the information contained in this book is accurate at the time of going to press, and the publishers and the author cannot accept responsibility for any errors or omissions, however caused. No responsibility for loss or damage occasioned to any person acting, or refraining from action, as a result of the material in this publication can be accepted by the publisher or the author.

About ISC

ISC is one of the first Certification Bodies to provide: Machine learning and developing and applying Artificial Intelligence Technology in all aspects of management system standards and certification services globally.

About ISC

ISC is a certification body that Provides certification services. ISC Publishes different educational books and provides educational courses and certification services. ISC operates under industry-approved international standards and requirements and maintains integrity and impartiality while taking into account professional and public interests. International Standard Certification (ISC) provides objective evidence that a person or an organization operates at the highest level of ethical, legal, professional, and technical standards.

ISC certifies a wide range of professionals and organizations, including governmental entities, commercial businesses, and professional associations. International Standard Certification (ISC) certification programs are based on recognized national and international compliance standards that ensure domestic and global acceptance.

International Credentials

International Standard Certification (ISC) is the leading skill development and certification body for professionals and organizations compliant with the ISO/IEC international standards that form a unified system for evaluating and recognizing competent certification bodies worldwide. As a global skill development and certification body, International Standard Certification (ISC) is committed to ensuring excellent service standards delivered by those we comply.

ISO/IEC is renowned for its rigorous compliance standards – influencing our approach to certify professionals and organizations, so we can serve you and your organization at the highest levels possible and positively influence your business results that would not happen otherwise.

International Standard Certification (ISC) Certified Professional Certification programs' chief goal is to be market-relevant, consensus-based, support innovation, and provide solutions to global challenges. That means thriving career chances for professionals, and meeting and exceeding demands from businesses and their valuable clients.

What Made Us Decide To Help Professionals?

Let us tell you this. The shock of getting fired helped us admit three very important things that we haven't been entirely honest ourselves before:

Large companies move slowly. Good ideas often died on the vine simply because they had to be approved by too many people.

Climbing the corporate ladder is an obstacle to doing great work. We wanted to focus on getting things done and making things better, not constantly positioning ourselves for promotion. Politics and turf wars are an inescapable part of the daily experience of working for a large company.

Frustration leads to burnout. We wanted to enjoy our daily work experience, but instead, We felt like We were running a gauntlet each day. It began to affect our health during working in happiness for all employees, friends, and family.

Why Did We Build The ISC?
We started the idea of ISC in 2009 with great knowledge of marketing, sales, persuasion, closing, e-commerce, and/or automated digital marketing systems. The more We learned, the more helpless We felt. For every great resource We found, I had to process ten other resources to figure out how to apply that resource in practice to excel on our own professional journey. We started to wonder: how much of what's out there —and there is a lot out there— We really needed to know. How could I separate practical business and professional skills from the dry theory and technobabble? We only had so much time and energy, so We started searching for a filter: something that would direct us to use skills and keep us away from the chaff. The more we searched, the more we realized it didn't exist — so we decided to create the International Standard Certification (ISC).

As of this moment, more than 5700 ISC Professionals, employees, employers, teachers, and schools, … are actively using International Standard Certification (ISC) Services, publications, educational books, certifications, and Training to quickly get their ideas, products, and services out to the world!

So take a deep breath. It's time for you to unlock the blueprint of success as a professional and get to work.

Welcome to the International Standard Certification (ISC)

About ISO

The International Organization for Standardization is an independent, non-governmental organization, the members of which are the standards organizations of the 165 member countries. It is the world's largest developer of voluntary international standards and it facilitates world trade by providing common standards among nations. More than twenty thousand standards have been set, covering everything from manufactured products and technology to food safety, agriculture, and healthcare. Use of the standards aids in the creation of products and services that are safe, reliable, and of good quality. The standards help businesses increase productivity while minimizing errors and waste. By enabling products from different markets to be directly compared, they facilitate companies in entering new markets and assist in the development of global trade on a fair basis. The standards also serve to safeguard consumers and the end-users of products and services, ensuring that certified products conform to the minimum standards set internationally.

History

The organization began in the 1920s as the International Federation of the National Standardizing Associations (ISA). It was suspended in 1942 during World War II, but after the war ISA was approached by the recently formed United Nations Standards Coordinating Committee (UNSCC) with a proposal to form a new global standards body. In October 1946, ISA and UNSCC delegates from 25 countries met in London and agreed to join forces to create the new International Organization for Standardization. The new organization officially began operations in February 1947.

Definitions

ISO 10002 serves as a comprehensive guideline for organizations in effectively managing customer complaints.

ISO 9001 is defined as the international standard that specifies requirements for a quality management system (QMS). Organizations use the standard to demonstrate the ability to consistently provide products and services that meet customer and regulatory requirements.

What is ISO 10002 standard?

The ISO 10002 standard outlines management controls and processes that help you to handle customer complaints more effectively and efficiently – making sure that more customers are satisfied with the service you provide.

What is the meaning of ISO certified? ISO certification is a seal of approval from a third party body that a company runs to one of the international standards developed and published by the International Organization for Standardization (ISO). ... ISO 9001 helps put your customers first.

ISO 10002 provides guidance on the process of complaints handling related to products within an organization, including planning, design, operation, maintenance and improvement.
The complaints-handling process described is suitable for use as one of the processes of an overall quality management system.

ISO 10002
Quality management
Customer satisfaction
Guidelines for complaints handling in organizations

What Are the Benefits of Being ISO 10002 Certified?

1 Boost Employee Performance and Productivity

2 Define Your Organization's Quality Control Processes

3 Improve Efficiency

4 Provide an Improved Customer Experience

5 Increase Confidence in your Products and/or Services

6 Cutting Costs

7 Less wastage

1: Boost Employee Performance and Productivity

Engaged employees are motivated to implement processes that are put in place to ensure that problems are quickly identified and resolved in a timely manner. Additionally, the consistent process audits through ISO 10002 can keep your employees focused while providing critical feedback when your processes deviate from consistency.

2: Define Your Organization's Quality Control Processes

A cornerstone component of ISO 10002 certification is establishing thorough business processes and defining responsibilities for quality control—and equally as important, relaying those specifications to employees. After all, 85% of employees are most motivated when internal communications are effective! Implementing ISO certification requirements provides valuable key performance metrics, such as on-time Services, throughput, and overall equipment effectiveness, to accurately reflect your system's performance. These metrics will help you make more educated decisions to improve growth and profitability throughout your Organization.

3: Improve Efficiency

Earning the ISO 10002 certification enforces a continuous improvement strategy, so that you're always, by design, seeking ways to reduce waste of (Energy and Time) and improve efficiency. Utilizing the requirements set forth in ISO 10002 will help to first identify areas of waste (Energy and Time) and then implement preventative measures to avoid Non conforming situations.

4: Provide an Improved Customer Experience

The ISO 10002 certification process provides an enhanced customer service experience by not only identifying key priorities for customers, but also outlining processes to further optimize these priorities based on customer expectations and needs. Services with enhanced quality translate into reduced customer complaints and more satisfied consumers. The most successful manufacturers of today know that delivering a better product experience is what will keep customers coming back. Providing a services in a way that reduces waste (Energy and Time) and cuts costs means that you can bring more value to your customer, which further reinforces their loyalty to your business.

5: Increase Confidence in your Products and/or Services

An ISO 10002 certification demonstrates to both customers and stakeholders that your business has the capabilities of delivering high-quality products and/or Services that meet all regulations and are delivered on time. This is crucial for your business, as your Services should reflect the measures taken to create consistency and confidence. An ISO 10002 certification also ensures that your business has all of the necessary tools, resources, and equipment for effectively providing your customer satisfaction service.

6: Cutting Costs

The quality management standard's process approach can also help your organisation reduce costs and increase profit. It does this by helping you: Optimise operations and improve the bottom line. Identify efficiencies and cost savings by monitoring and analysing process interactions.

7: Less Wastage

Earning the ISO 10002 certification enforces a continuous improvement strategy, so that you're always, by design, seeking ways to reduce waste and improve efficiency. Utilizing the requirements set forth in ISO 10002 will help to first identify areas of waste and then implement preventative measures to avoid wasteful situations. Streamlining your manufacturing operations from the ground up through ISO 10002 means every moving part is as effective as possible rather than discarded or unused.

Introduction to Quality Management System (QMS)

What is Quality ?
How would you describe what "Quality" means ?

Degree to which a set of inherent characteristics fulfils requirements

QUALITY DOES NOT OCCUR BY ACCIDENT

Identify, understand and agree customer requirements

Plan to achieve them

Measure, monitor & control processes/activities

REQUIRES A SYSTEM

Understanding the Customer's Requirements

Which is better, Customer Satisfaction and/or Delighting your Customers?

Gain complete visibility into customer experience metrics to transform your business. Deliver innovative experiences by collecting actionable customer insights. Multilingual Support. Tailored solutions. Capture Customer Profiles. Engage Your Customers.

QUALITY DOES NOT OCCUR BY ACCIDENT

REQUIRES A SYSTEM

Identify, understand and agree customer requirements
Plan to achieve them
Measure, monitor & control processes/activities

7 Ways to Amaze and Delight Your Customers

Always Try to Do Better. ...
Anticipate Customer Needs. ...
Deliver Beyond Customer Expectations. ...
Be Consistent Across Channels. ... Continually Ensure Your customers Value What you Offer. ...
Eliminate Dissatisfaction (So You Can Focus on Loyalty) ...
Empathize with Customers. ...
Empower your Employees.

General
Identify processes, based on the following approch:

INPUT ●⟶ PROCESS ●⟶ OUTPUT

Determine sequence and interaction, Measure Monitor and Analyse

Documentation requirements

Documented procedures required by this standard and those needed by the organisation to control its processes. The extent of the QMS documentation depends on the following:

a) size and type of the organisation
b) complexity and interaction of the processes
c) competence of personnel

Secret of Effective Management System Documentation

When you develop any documentation, verify it with the follwoing rules:

5 W's and 1 H

If your document can answer these 6 questions, then you have developed a completely effective document; no matter that it is a quality manual, procedure, SOP, work instruction,.......

Who, When, Where, Why, What and How

Who	Customers, Employees, Suppliers, Competitors, Govenrment
What	Strategy (Corporate, Business Unit, Marketing Product)
Where	Markets, Facilities, Distribution, Outsourcing
When	Strategic Plan. Annual Plan, Proogram and Projct Management
Why	Leadership, Communities, Culture, Change management
How	Marketing, Operating Plan, Sales Force, Metrtics, Incentives

Quality Manual

Establish & maintain a manual including:
scope of QMS with details/justification
for any exclusions
procedures or reference to them
description of sequence and interaction
of processes included in QMS

What should a quality manual include?

As a Quality Manual is the same as a user manual of an equipment so the comparisons are as follow:

Use Manual of an Equipment	a Quality Manual
Introduction	Introduction of organization
Contents	Contents
a Detailed Photo of Parts	Organizational Chart
Description of Parts	Duties and Responsibilities
Meeting Needs	Meeting requirements of Standard

Don't forget that the "Standard" is a Question Book and the "Quality Manual" is an Answer Book, thus repeating the sentences of standards for each clause in the quality manual shows that the writer did not understand the concept of the minimum requirements for the quality management systems.

Time Frame	Task
Day 1	GAP Analysis Certification Body Selection Cost Estimates
Week 1	Developing Documents
Week 4	Implementing Management System
Week 8	Internal Audit MRM CAPA
Week 10	Certification Body Audit N-C Closing
Week 12	Certificate Issued
Year on Year	Yearly Compliance

	Process
	Finding the GAP between existing system related to ISO requirements Selecting the appropriate certification body Based on the scope of your business & certification body you choose
	Management System Manual, Management System Procedures, Policy, Objectives, Forms etc. Review of Standard Operating Procedures (SOP)
	ISO Awareness training for the top management and staff Implementing a well-documented management system throughout the organization
	Internal audits identifying nonconformities related to ISO requirements Management Review Meetings Corrective and Preventive Action plan for nonconformities
	ISC acts on your behalf and assists you in the third-party audit Closing of any nonconformities identified by the certification body
	ISO certificates issued for 3 years Surveillance Audits yearly
	Support of Yearly documentation for audit

Control of Documents

QMS documents shall be controlled.
A documented procedure shall be established:
 to approve documents prior to use
 to review/update & re-approve as necessary
 to identify changes and current revision status
 to ensure relevant versions are available
 to ensure legibility and identification
 to control documents of external origin
 to control obsolete documents

Don't be afraid of the above mentioned requirements, you can meet all of these needs via the following EASY solutions:

- Create an account in one of the online drives with enough capacity of the volume of your documentation, usually 100 Gb is enough.
- Create a file system directory for keeping your manual and procedures there and giving share access to authorized persons and assign a person as administration. Then they shall take care that it's always an updated version of documents are online and obsolete documents are out of access.

Control of Records

QMS records shall be maintained to provide evidence of conformance to requirements and effective QMS operation.

A documented procedure shall be established for : Identification, storage, retrieval, protection, retention time and disposition of records.

Don't Afraid of the above mentiond requirements, you can meet all of these needs via the following EASY solutions:

Records are the result of implementation of a system, So they are the most important objective evidences that show the performance of the system.

You can do the same as using documents for controlling the records. For some paper items, please scan and upload in appropriate drive.

Management Review

Review QMS at planned intervals to ensure suitability and effectiveness.

Review input:
- results of audits
- customer feedback
- process performance & product conformance
- status of preventive & corrective actions
- actions from earlier management reviews
- changes that could affect the QMS
- recommendations for improvemen

Management Review

Outputs from management review shall include decisions and actions related to:
- Improvement of the QMS and its processes
- Improvement of product related to customer requirements
- Resource needs
- Results of management reviews shall be recorded

The system is working for you (the system is fully integrated along your processes and eases your operations).

You are working for the system (the system is beside your operations and looks as an additional burden.)

Here is a famous fable of an elephant and six blind men used as a metaphor. This picture conveys that different people will look at the standard in their own subjective-way. It is also used illustrate that different people in an organization will have different perceptions of risks and opportunities that the organization needs to address at any given time.

The Most Important Clause: Preventive Actions

- Identify action to prevent potential nonconformities
- documented procedure
- determine potential problems and their causes
- evaluate need for action
- implement preventive action
- record results of action taken
- review action taken

Bibliography

Bibliography:

Anttila, J., & Jussila, K. (2017). ISO 9001:2015- a questionable reform. What should the implementing organisations understand and do? Total Quality Management and Business Excellence, 28(9-10), 1090-1105. https://doi.org/10.1080/14783363.2017.1309119.

Astrini, N. (2018). ISO 9001 and performance: a method review. Total Quality Management & Business Excellence, doi: 10.1080/14783363.2018.1524293.

Bou-Llusar, J. C., Escrig-Tena, A. B., Roca-Puig, V., & Beltrán-Martín, I. (2005). To what extent do enablers explain results in the EFQM excellence model? International Journal of Quality & Reliability Management, 22(44), 337-353.

Chatzoglou, P., Chatzoudes, D., & Kipraios, N. (2015). The impact of ISO 9000 certification on firms' financial performance. International Journal of Operations and Production Management, 35(1), 145-174. https://doi.org/10.1108/IJOPM-07-2012-0387

Chiarini, A. (2017). Risk-based thinking according to ISO 9001:2015 standard and the risk sources European manufacturing SMEs intend to manage. The TQM Journal, 29(2), 310-323. https://doi.org/10.1108/TQM-04-2016-0038.

Domingues, J. P. T., Sampaio, P., & Arezes, P. M. (2016). Integrated management systems assessment: a maturity model proposal. Journal of Cleaner Production, 124, 164-174, doi: 10.1016/j.jclepro.2016.02.103

Gigante, N., & Ziantoni, S. (2015). L'edizione 2015 della norma ISO 9001, 2015. Retrieved from:https://www.accredia.it/app/uploads/2015/12/6050_5_L__700_edizione_2015_della_norma_ISO_9001___Arch__Gigante__Dr__Ziantoni.pdf

ISO (2015a). ISO 9001 - Quality management systems – requirements. Geneva: International Organization for Standardization, ISO 10002,

ISO (2015). ISO Survey 2015 (online). Retrieved from: http//www.iso.org.

ISO (2018). ISO 19011 - Guidelines for auditing management systems quality management systems. Geneva: International Organization for Standardization.

ISO (2019). ISO 9000 Family - Quality Management. Retrieved from: https://www.iso.org/home.html.

Wilson, J. P., & Campbell, L. (2018). ISO 9001:2015: the evolution and convergence of quality management and knowledge management for competitive advantage. Total Quality Management and Business Excellence, pp. 1-16. https://doi.org/10.1080/ 14783363.2018.1445965

ISC
INTERNATIONAL STANDARD CERTIFICATION

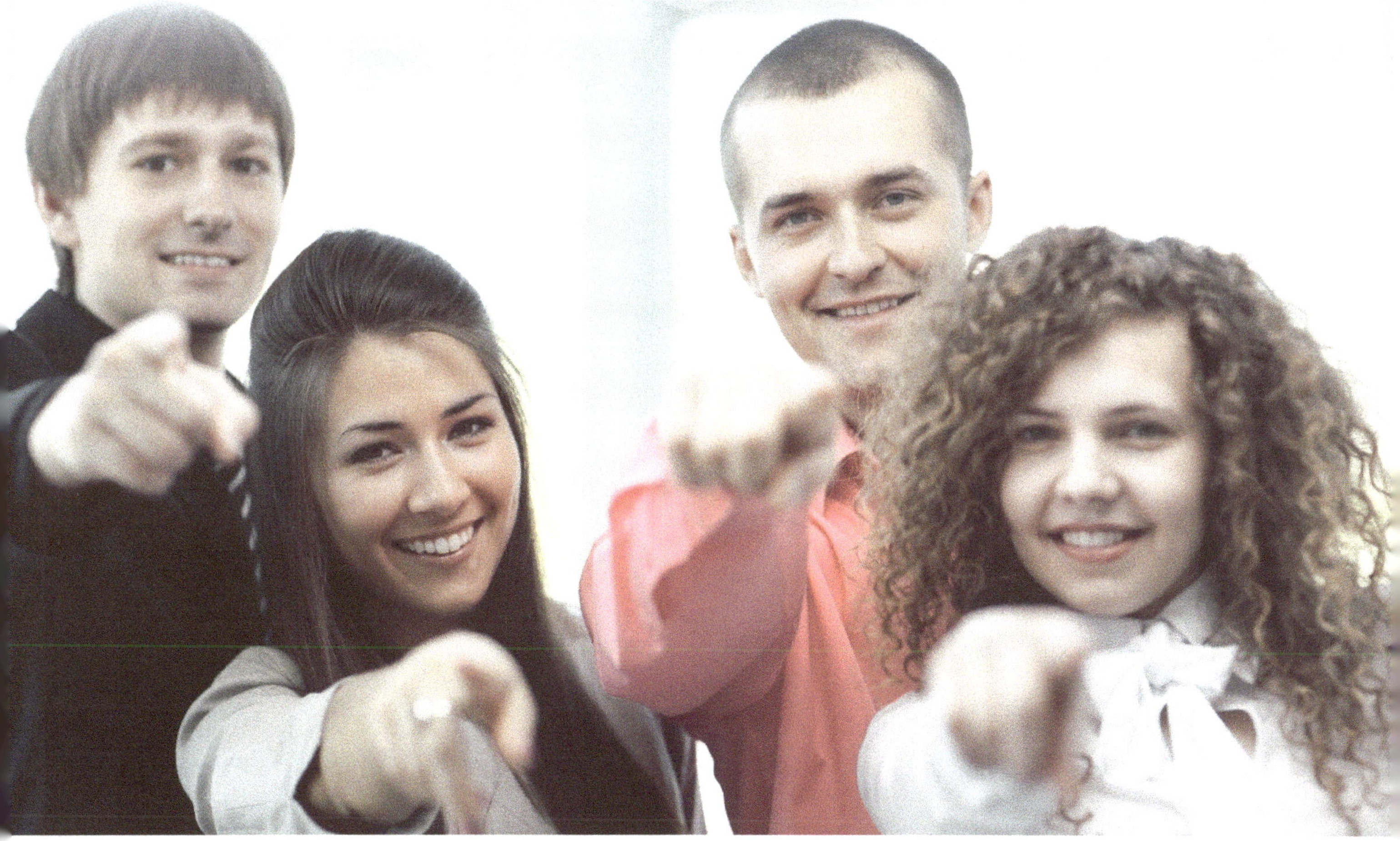

WWW.ISCASC.COM   Vol.1, No.011   **2024**

ISC ARTIFICIAL INTELIGENCE MAGAZINE

>CONTENTS

ISC One of the first Certification Bodies to provide: Machine learning & Developing and applying Artificial Intelligence Technology

03	**LEADERSHIP TAM** We have to be flexible enough to adapt our leadership
04	**A NOTE FROM CEO** ISC is one of the first certification bodies to provide
06	**AI ENABLED MEDICAL DEVICES** is rising, FDA Authorization
08	**Q+A WHY ISC** What is the purpose of ISC Certification
10	**CLIMATE CHANGE CONROL** We hope that 10,000 years from now,...
13	**ISC ONLINE TRAINING** How to ensure your virtual training sessions make ...
14	**ENVIRONMENTAL LABELLING** is a voluntary method of environmental
17	**ISC INTERNATIONAL** Integrated medical equipment audit program
18	**OUR SERVICES** International Management System Standards
20	**APPLYING FOR** ISO 10002 Certification
22	**ISC REPRESENTATIVE** Offices from around the world
24	**ISC CANADA** In conclusion, while preventive action may indeed present
26	**MOST RECENT** Countries to join ISC

WWW.ISCASC.COM – SPRING 2024

INTERNATIONAL **STANDARD** CERTIFICATION

> GLOBAL LEADERSHIP TEAM

We have to be flexible enough to adapt our leadership style to the certification services that we're working with."
Respect different cultures.

WWW.ISCASC.COM – SPRING 2024

ISC ARTIFICIAL INTELIGENCE MAGAZINE

A NOTE FROM OUR
CEO

 ISC is one of the first Certification Bodies to provide: Machine learning and developing and applying Artificial Intelligence Technology.

ISC is a certification body that Provides certification services. ISC Publishes different educational books and provides educational courses and certification services. ISC operates under industry-approved international standards and requirements and maintains integrity and impartiality while taking into account professional and public interests. International Standard Certification (ISC) provides objective evidence that a person or an organization operates at the highest level of ethical, legal, professional, and technical standards.

ISC certifies a wide range of professionals and organizations, including governmental entities, commercial businesses, and professional associations. International Standard Certification (ISC) certification programs are based on recognized national and international compliance standards that ensure domestic and global acceptance.

International Standard Certification (ISC) is the leading skill development and certification body for professionals and organizations compliant with the ISO/IEC international standards that form a unified system for evaluating and recognizing competent certification bodies worldwide. As a global skill development and certification body, International Standard Certification (ISC) is committed to ensuring excellent service standards delivered by those we comply.

ISO/IEC is renowned for its rigorous compliance standards – influencing our approach to certify professionals and organizations, so we can serve you and your organization at the highest levels possible and positively influence your business results that would not happen otherwise.

International Standard Certification (ISC) Certified Professional Certification programs' chief goal is to be market-relevant, consensus-based, support innovation, and provide solutions to global challenges. That means thriving career chances for professionals, and meeting and exceeding demands from businesses and their valuable clients. Let us tell you this. The shock of getting fired helped us admit three very important things that we haven't been entirely honest ourselves before: Large companies move slowly. Good ideas often died on the vine simply because they had to be approved by too many people. Climbing the corporate ladder is an obstacle to doing great work. We wanted to focus on getting things done and making things better, not constantly positioning ourselves for promotion. Politics and turf wars are an inescapable part of the daily experience of working for a large company.

We started the idea of ISC in 2009 with great knowledge of marketing, sales, persuasion, closing, e-commerce, and/or automated digital marketing systems. The more We learned, the more helpless We felt. For every great resource We found, I had to process ten other resources to figure out how to apply that resource in practice to excel on our own professional journey.

The more we searched, the more we realized it didn't exist – so we decided to create the International Standard Certification (ISC). As of this moment, more than 5700 ISC Professionals, employees, employers, teachers, and schools, … are actively using International Standard Certification (ISC) Services, publications, educational books, certifications, and Training to quickly get their ideas, products, and services out to the world!

So take a deep breath. It's time for you to unlock the blueprint of success as a professional and get to work. Welcome to the **International Standard Certification (ISC)**

INTERNATIONAL **STANDARD** CERTIFICATION

YOUR LOCAL, REGIONAL AND INTERNATIONAL SOURCE OF MANAGEMENT SYSTEMS.

International Standard Certification
ISC is one of the first Certification Bodies to provide: Machine learning and developing and applying Artificial Intelligence Technology in all aspects of management system standards.

> ISC headquarter located in Vancouver, CANADA, with more than 77 representatives in different countries globally.

ISC Vision: Upgrading International Standardization of Developing countries through Training programs empower young people with skills, knowledge and providing a great framework of standardization worldwide by implementing encouraging programs for recognizing National Industrial, Artificial Intelligence products and services at Regional and International level.

WWW.ISCASC.COM — SPRING 2021

AI ENABLED MEDICAL DEVICE IS RISING, FDA AUTHORIZATION

ISC HELP YOU TO UPDATE YOUR ISO 13485 CERTIFICATION

AI Quality Management for Medical Device Companies

THE FOOD AND DRUG ADMINISTRATION RELEASED A NEW ACCOUNTING OF ARTIFICIAL INTELLIGENCE TOOLS CLEARED FOR USE IN HEALTHCARE, ADDING SCORES OF NEW PRODUCTS DESIGNED TO RESHAPE CARE IN SEVERAL AREAS OF MEDICINE.

The Food and Drug Administration released a new accounting of **artificial intelligence** tools cleared for use in health care, adding scores of new products designed to reshape care in several areas of medicine.

The update included more than 200 new products that use artificial intelligence and machine learning, including 177 authorized since August of 2022. The agency's data indicate that, after a lull during the Covid-19 pandemic, the number of authorized devices in 2023 and 2024 is expected to increase by more than 35% over the prior year..

An important next step in our AI journey would be updating ISO management system documentation and certification processes and ISC International Standard Certification, is one of the leaders starting huge activities in this regards.

If you would like to receive more details, please visit our website: www.ISCASC.com.

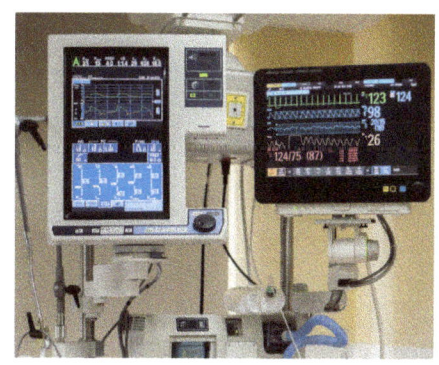

ISC ARTIFICIAL INTELIGENCE MAGAZINE

Q+A

WHY ISC

Interview by Johnathan Ive
Image provided by Equestre and Build Source

WHAT IS THE PURPOSE OF ISC CERTIFICATE?

WHAT IS THE DIFFERENCE BETWEEN ISC AND OTHER CONFORMITY ASSESSMENT ORGANIZATIONS?

WHY GET CERTIFIED TO ISC ARTIFICIAL INTELIGENCE STANDARDS?

Q What is the purpose of ISC Certificate?

Achieving a **ISC** certification means your company's products and/or services have attained the requirements of related standards e.g. safety, quality, Environment and sustainability. This gives resellers and partners the confidence to work with you and consumers the peace of mind to use your products.

Q What is the difference between ISC and other conformity assessment organizations?

A ISC is a North American based certification body with the follwoing exclusive specifications:

ISC is one of the first Certification Bodies to provide: Machine learning and developing and applying Artificial Intelligence Technology in all aspects of management system standards and certification services globally.

ISC is the most important developer of International Standards regarding the application of Artifial Intelligence in all aspect of management systems.

WWW.ISCASC.COM – SPRING 2024

INTERNATIONAL STANDARD CERTIFICATION

> **Our Signature for your S U C C E S S**

ISC certified companies benefits: Improved business process efficiency, Sustainability, Reduced expenses, improved communication and corporate culture, innovation and risk reduction.

Exclusive membership for an important Canadian network titled: Top Ten Award International Network. This helps all individuals and businesses who are interested in residing in Canada and/or doing business in Canada.

ISC certified company's details will be published in publicly available databases, books & magazines accessible on more than 40,000 websites in more than 75 countries..

Q How ISC certification helps to increase profits of my organization?

A ISC Certification give you access to internationally recognized best practices across your business. Standards exist for everything from quality management to environmental performance, information security, food safety, risk management, and health and safety.

Q How long does it take to achieve ISC Certification?

A ISC Certification may take between 3-6 months, depending on the complexity and size of the business and the requested standard. For instance, companies with less than ten employees can take up to 3 months to achieve an ISO 9001 and/or ISO 10002 Quality & Customer satisfaction Management System certification.

WWW.ISCASC.COM – SPRING 2024

ISC ARTIFICIAL INTELIGENCE MAGAZINE

International Manual of
CLIMATE CHANGE CONTROL
Save the Earth

Professional Environment & Food Quality Technologist with a master's degree in Science and a PhD in Environmental & Quality Sciences; International Certification and Lead Auditor in ISO/IEC 17025, ISO 19011, ISO 9001, ISO 14000, ISO 45001. Participated in more than 110 audits in more than 25 countries, responsible for planning, developing, initiating, coordinating, implementing, and maintaining the most effective eco-labelling and environmental management systems dedicated to both farm production, food quality, environmental assurance, and monitoring and measurement in more than 11 countries. One of the first people to suggest to ISO the use of mobile phones as management system tools for recognized innovative behavior. After three-year's hardest working finalizing 'Manual of Climate change control and now it is printing in more than 10 thousands copies outside Canada and distributed in more than 17 countries **as a text book of secondary schools** accompanying with online knowledge test and certification from Canada.

We hope that, 10,000 years from now, future generations will be able to see flowers that provide bees with nectar and pollen and… BEES provide flowers with the means to reproduce byBEES by Spreading pollen from flower to flower… Jahangir Asadi

Why Climate Change Control?

Recycling conserves natural resources, reduces pollution and saves energy Everyone can help limit climate change. From the way we travel, to the electricity we use and the food we eat, we can make a difference. Start with these twelve actions to help tackle the climate crisis. Humans and wild animals face new challenges for survival because of climate change. More frequent and intense drought, storms, heat waves, rising sea levels, melting glaciers and warming oceans can directly harm animals, destroy the places they live, and wreak havoc on people's livelihoods and communities.

Overall, glaciers are melting at a faster rate. Sea ice in the Arctic Ocean around the North Pole is melting faster with the warmer temperatures. Permafrost is melting, releasing methane, a powerful greenhouse gas, into the atmosphere. Sea levels are rising, threatening coastal communities and estuarine ecosystems.

This Full Color manual dedicated to 'Environmental Sustain for Future Kids' for a sustainable living education. ISC, TTAIN & ESFK improves quality of life and reduces environmental degradation by fostering new consumption patterns and sustainable lifestyles through International Cooperative Extension Service programs at houses, offices, schools and libraries all over the globe.

INTERNATIONAL STANDARD CERTIFICATION

Food Safety and-or HACCP?
by: N.Waezi & J.Asadi

This EASY-to-understand book is ideal for all (Employees & Employers) and other people who are new to HACCP, ISO 22000, (International Standard) who want to get more out of an established Quality Management System (QMS). Particularly for employees who just need a basic understanding of what HACCP is and how it applies to them. This Book was written so that anyone at any level of the organization can get to the heart of the standard's requirements and how they apply to the organization quickly and simply.

ISC Publication Department: Work with ISC talented publishing team to design, edit, distribute and market professional books, Standards, Manuals, ... We are an experienced and friendly team of publishing professionals dedicated to providing authors with an exceptional publishing experience. Recognizing the confusion and quandaries often associated with the industry, our consultative approach aims to guide and empower authors at every step of the process.

Founded in 2017 in Vancouver, British Columbia, ISC emerged to address a noticeable gap in the assisted Standardization sector. Observing that major management system standards training materials , user friendly and easy to understand by all employees.

MDD VS MDR The European Union's regulatory landscape for medical devices has undergone a significant transformation with the transition from the Medical Device Directive (MDD) to the Medical Device Regulation (MDR). This shift has profound implications for legal manufacturers, affecting everything from product development to post-market surveillance. Understanding these changes is crucial to ensure regulatory compliance and successful market access. The **MDD**, officially known as Directive 93/42/EEC, was the previous framework governing medical devices in the European Union. As a directive, it set out the goals that EU countries should achieve, but allowed for some flexibility in how they implemented the rules. This flexibility led to variations in how the rules were applied across different countries, creating inconsistencies in the regulatory landscape. The **MDR**, officially known as EU 2017/745, replaced the MDD in May 2021.

Unlike the MDD, the MDR is a regulation, meaning it is directly applicable in all EU countries without the need for national legislation. This ensures a more uniform application of the rules across all EU countries, enhancing the overall consistency and transparency of the regulatory framework. **ISC Canada** is finalizing a comprehensive transition guide from MDD to MDR, set to be available internationally next month. Key Changes :
* Expanded Definition of Medical Devices
* Enhanced Post-Market Surveillance
* Introduction of UDI System
* Person responsible for Regulatory Compliance
* Rigorous Clinical Evaluation

MDSAP Certification

A complete guide (487 Pages) with sample checklists, This EASY-to-understand book is ideal for all (Employees & Employers) and other people who are new to MDSAP, ISO 13485, (International Standard) who want to get more out of an established Quality Management System (QMS). Particularly for employees who just need a basic understanding of what MDSAP is and how it applies to them. This Book was written so that anyone at any level of the organization can get to the heart of the standard's requirements and how they apply to the organization quickly and simply. This book is available in more than 39,000 bookstores globally.

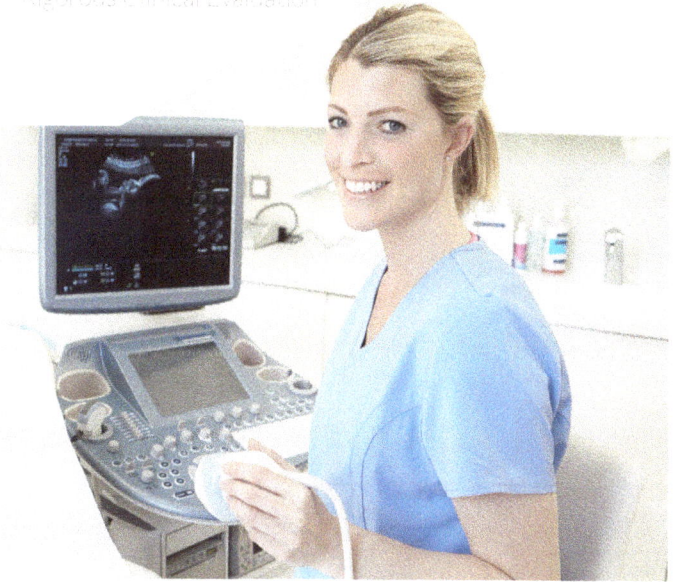

WWW.ISCASC.COM - SPRING 2024

ONLINE TRAINING
TRAIN.ISCASC.COM
AI ENABLED

CLIMATE CHANGE CONTROL & ENV. LABELING ....

PROUDLY CANADIAN - PROUDLY CANADIAN

Join the 17,000+ organizations around the globe that proudly trust ISC Training portal

ISC Online Training Courses Certification

- Easy session management
- More learning engagement
- An AI integrated journey
- Learning insights

Access pre-packaged integrations with your favorite video platforms, including Microsoft Teams, Zoom, WebEx, and more.

Tel: 1-877-307-3077

www.iscasc.com

Hq. Office: Vancouver, BC **CANADA**

How to ensure your virtual training sessions make an impact

Virtual meeting integrations

ISC ARTIFICIAL INTELIGENCE MAGAZINE

ENVIRONMENTAL LABELLING

Ecolabelling is a voluntary method of environmental performance certification and labelling that is practised around the world.

> The volumes series books are dedicated to the subject of environmental labels. The basis for the classification of its texts goes back to the types of environmental labeling according to the classifications provided by the International Organization for standardization. In each section, we're presenting the relevant definitions, I'venth in the existing International standards and present examples related to each type of labelling. Environmental labelling is an important and significant topic, and its richness is added to every day, which has attracted the attention of many experts and researchers around the world. The idea of compiling this book, came to my mind when I observed that national environmental labeling moulds have been successful in most countries of the world, but in many other countries, the initial steps have not been taken yet. Therefore, I decided to create the first spark for the development of environmental labeling patterns in other countries by collecting appropriate materials and inserting samples of labelling patterns of different countries of the world.

> **ISO 14024:2018** also establishes the certification procedures for awarding the label.

> **ISO 14024:2018** establishes the principles and procedures for developing Type I environmental labelling programmes, including the selection of product categories, product environmental criteria and product function characteristics, and for assessing and demonstrating compliance.

> **ISC International**
We hereby ask all interested parties around the world who wish to start an environmental labelling program in their country to benefit from our intellectual assistance and support in the form of consulting contracts.

WWW.ISCASC.COM – SPRING 2024

INTERNATIONAL **STANDARD** CERTIFICATION

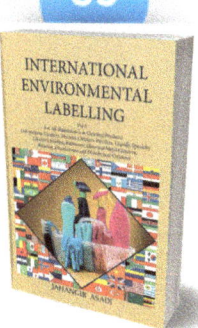

WWW.ISCASC.COM – SPRING 2024

ISC
INTERNATIONAL STANDARD

Integrated medical equipment audit program: The "Integrated Medical Device Audit Program" process, abbreviated as **MDSAP**, has been designed and developed to ensure that all medical device requirements are audited with a single audit.

What is MDSAP? MDSAP is an international audit program based on a model designed by the International Association of Medical Device Regulators (IMDRF) with the participation of relevant regulatory bodies from five countries: the United States Food and Drug Administration (FDA), the Canadian Ministry of Health, the Australian Ministry of Health (TGA), the Brazilian Ministry of Health (ANVISA) and the Japanese Ministry of Health (MHLW). The United States leads the way in the number of MDSAP certifications, but the past year has seen steady adoption in markets such as Brazil. The European Union is currently working out the details of implementing this with one among its member states and has not yet joined. The MDSAP audit sequence was designed and developed to enable audits to be conducted in a logical, focused and efficient manner. The MDSAP audit sequence follows a process approach and has four core processes and one support process. These processes include the following: (1) Management, (2) measure, analyze and improve; (3) design and development, (4) production and service controls and (5) Purchase.

INTERNATIONAL **STANDARD** CERTIFICATION

Medical Device Manufacturing Everything You Need to: MDSAP, CE Mark, ISO 13485, FDA, Health Canada & Regulatory Affairs

Manufacturers across the board are waking up to the potential of servitizing previously product-oriented businesses, building out their book of business with service and outcomes-based solutions. For manufacturers who build and sell medical devices, the opportunity is certainly just as apparent.

While some customers expect systems and assets to work as expected, medical workers often require uninterrupted utilization in order to keep their patients safe and meet the unique day-to-day challenges that they face.

Issues need to be resolved quickly, and service technicians need to work around the diverse, and often inconsistent needs of the business. Getting this right is a daunting task, but one that certainly pays dividends. It starts with a smart approach to technology and a solution-oriented mindset.

For many medical device companies considering how service technology fits into their business, they naturally assume that custom implementations will ultimately be required in order to meet the demands of a complex and bespoke type of manufacturer. The truth is, though, that smart service management software is designed to be configured to the contours of your business, rather than requiring the time and complexities that come along with customization. To get this right, it's important to focus on the right set of capabilities for your business. There are invariably a huge variety that are worth considering, but based on what we've seen, there are some common challenges that can be remedied with powerful solutions. ISC like to pick elements from each stage of the service lifecycle to frame some key capabilities around.

WWW.ISCASC.COM – SPRING 2024

ISC ARTIFICIAL INTELIGENCE MAGAZINE

OUR SERVICES

ISO 9001

QUALITY M.S.

The ISO 9001 standard is an international quality management standard that is applicable to any type of organization in any sector or activity and, regardless of its size, due to its great flexibility, it is fully compatible with the management characteristics of any existing company. ISO 9001 is the most extensive and applicable global standard.

ISC AI

ISC.

One of the first Certification Bodies to provide:

Machine learning & Developing and applying

Artificial Intelligence Technology in all aspects of management system standards and certification services globally.

ISO 27001

ISO/IEC 27001 is the international standard for information security management. Part of the ISO 27000 series, ISO 27001 sets out a framework for all organisations to establish, implement, operate, monitor, review, maintain ...

ISO 14001

The ISO14001 standard is about environmental management to help companies and institutions

CE MARK

All about new CE mark regulations.

MDD 2 MDR

GETTING TO KNOW THE NEW CE MARK REGULATIONS!

In Europe Region, there is the MDD (Medical Devices Directive) as well as MDR (Medical Device Regulation). Understanding the MDD vs MDR difference is vital for manufacturers to safely carry out their operations in European countries.

ISO 13485

ISO 13485 certification (quality management system in medical equipment) focuses on a quality management system in the design, development, production, assembly, after-sales service and distribution of all types of medical equipment and makes the process of obtaining the CE mark easy for export to Europe.

INTERNATIONAL **STANDARD** CERTIFICATION

HACCP

HACCP is one of the methods of monitoring the quality of the food industry, in which the quality of the food industry is examined from the production stage to the final purchase.

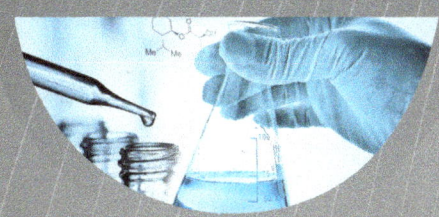

HEALTH CANADA

WHAT IS ESTABLISHMENT IN CANADA?!

Definition. Establishment refers to the level in the statistical hierarchy below the company in the Business Register statistical hierarchy, and at which the accounting data required to measure production are available (principal inputs, revenues, salaries and wages).

ISO 22000

ISO 22000 is a Food Safety Management System that can be applied to any organization in the food chain, farm to fork.

FDA

USA FDA

US FDA Medical Device Establishment Registration and FURLS Listing. Any establishment involved in the production, importation, reprocessing/relabeling, or developing specifications of a medical device or IVD for commercial sale in the United States must register annually with the US Food and Drug Administration (FDA).

MDSAP

AUSTRALIA, BRAZIL, CANADA, JAPAN, USA

The Medical Device Single Audit Program allows an MDSAP recognized Auditing Organization to conduct a single regulatory audit of a medical device manufacturer that satisfies the relevant requirements of the regulatory authorities participating in the program.

ISO 50001

Designed to support organizations in all sectors, this ISO standard provides a practical way to improve energy use, through the development

ISO 45001

SUB HEADING

Ntus tebatratil tem hali, perfica toratumus inat, cendi potatus eto cus vividet veret avessimulut faus me it de in huid corarbis et int. Os ad ret, us viris, catum.

ISO 26000

It provides guidance to those who recognize that respect for society and environment is a critical success factor. As well as being the "right thing" to do,

WWW.ISCASC.COM – SPRING 2024

> Customer satisfaction is old-fashioned,
> You have to try to delight your customers,
> effectively and you'll have more chance of
> meeting their expectations as well .

APPLYING FOR
ISO 10002 CERTIFICATION

What is ISO 10002 Customer Satisfaction. Complaints Handling?

Customers expect more and more from the service you provide. And your competitors are working harder to meet these expectations. You can too with ISO 10002, the international standard of measures to improve customer satisfaction. It provides you with guidelines for putting in place your own complaints management system – helping you to identify complaints, their cause and how to eliminate them. ISO 10002 will also allow you to identify areas in your business where you can improve and eventually remove the cause of complaints. The standard outlines management controls and processes that help you to handle customer complaints more effectively and efficiently – making sure that more customers are satisfied with the service you provide. ISO 10002, gives guidelines for the process of complaints handling related to products and services within an organization, including planning, design, development, operation, maintenance and improvement. The complaints-handling process described is suitable for use as one of the processes of an overall quality management system.

- Achieve operational efficiency to identify trends and causes of complaints
- Resolve more complaints by adopting a more customer-focused approach
- Engage staff with new customer service training opportunities
- Integrate ISO 10002 with ISO 9001 to improve overall efficiency

Monitor and continually improve your complaints handling process. octo ium iam intre num mur, conte islo abit, patua non num am. Publiuchus tam.

HOW TO GET CERTIFIED TO ISO 10002 BY ISC?

We make the certification process simple. After you apply we appoint a client manager who will guide you and your business through the following steps.

ISC Gap analysis

This is an optional service where ISC take a closer look at your existing complaints management system and compare it with ISO 10002 requirements. This helps identify areas that need more work before we carry out a formal assessment, saving you time and money.

ISC Formal assessment

This happens in two stages. First we review your organization's preparedness for assessment by checking if the necessary ISO 10002 procedures and controls have been developed. ISC will share the details of

INTERNATIONAL STANDARD

our findings with you so that if we find holes, you can close them. If all the requirements are in place, we will then assess the implementation of the procedures and controls within your organization to make sure that they are working effectively as required for certification.

ISC Certification

When you have passed the formal assessment you will receive an ISO 10002 certificate, which is valid for three years. Your client manager will stay in touch during this time, visiting you regularly to make sure your system doesn't just remain compliant, but that it continually improves.

❝ **ALWAYS LISTEN TO YOUR CUSTOMERS. THEY HAVE COMPLAINED FOR A REASON AND IT IS IMPORTANT TO UNDERSTAND WHY THEY ARE COMPLAINING.** ❞

When customers call to register a complaint and discover that their input was taken into consideration and changes were implemented, they will be pleased to know that their opinions were considered. Many customers avoid filing complaints or expressing their concerns because they assume businesses do not care and will not take action. When you act the contrary and demonstrate that you've listened to them and that their satisfaction is a priority, your clients will recognize that your communication channels are genuinely "open" and not only for effect.

ISC REPRESENTATIVE OFFICES FROM AROUND THE WORLD

Interested in becoming our representative?
Drop us an email to:
REP@ISCASC.COM

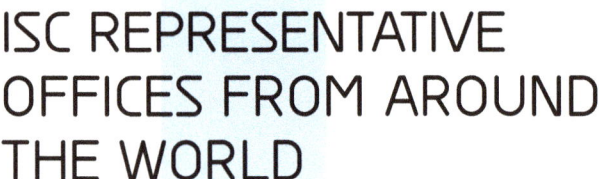

ISC ARTIFICIAL INTELIGENCE MAGAZINE

ISC CANADA

> *In conclusion, while preventive action may indeed present challenges, its strategic value cannot be overstated.*

HQ VANCOUVER, BC CANADA

CHANGING THE WAY

Prevantive action: the greatest weakness

Two different certification style: **A.** *The system is working for you (the system is fully integrated along your processes and eases your operations).* **B.** *You are working for the system (the system is beside your operations and looks as an additional burden.)*

THE CHALLENGE OF PREVENTIVE ACTION IN BUSINESS

In the realm of business strategy, preventive action often stands as a paradoxical challenge—its importance widely acknowledged, yet its execution frequently faltering. The concept of preventive action revolves around anticipating and mitigating risks before they escalate into significant issues. While intuitively sound, its implementation across various industries reveals inherent complexities and shortcomings.

At its core, preventive action embodies a proactive approach to risk management. It aims to pre-emptively identify potential threats to business continuity, operational efficiency, or reputation and implement measures to either eliminate or mitigate these risks. This proactive stance contrasts with reactive approaches, which address problems after they have manifested, often resulting in greater costs and disruptions.

One of the primary obstacles to effective preventive action lies in the difficulty of accurately predicting future risks. Business environments are dynamic, influenced by numerous factors such as technological advancements, regulatory changes, economic shifts, and unforeseen events like pandemics or geopolitical tensions. Despite sophisticated risk assessment tools and methodologies, the sheer complexity and interconnectedness of these variables can challenge even the most diligent risk managers. Moreover, there exists a psychological barrier within organizations where immediate, tangible results often take precedence over long-term preventive measures. This short-termism can lead businesses to prioritize operational efficiency and profitability in the present moment, neglecting investments in risk prevention that may not yield immediate visible returns. Furthermore, the effectiveness of preventive action hinges significantly on organizational culture and leadership commitment. A culture that values transparency, accountability, and continuous improvement is more likely to foster a proactive approach to risk management. Conversely, hierarchical structures, communication silos, and a lack of cross-functional collaboration can impede the timely identification and response to emerging risks.

> ISC ARTIFICIAL INTELIGENCE MAGAZINE

MOST RECENT COUNTRIES TO JOIN

OMAN

Attention Business Professionals: Represent Our Canadian Company!

ISC International Standard Certification, ISC is one of the first certification bodies to provide machine learning and develop and apply Artificial Intelligence Technology in all aspects of management system standards and certification services globally.

Are you a motivated and experienced business owner looking to represent a Canadian company? We're seeking dedicated corporations to serve as our exclusive representatives in various countries.

Requirements:
- Must be a business owner with an incorporated company.
- Demonstrated experience in sales, marketing, or related fields.
- Strong communication and negotiation skills.
- Familiarity with management system standards ISO (e.g., ISO 9001, ISO 14001).
- Ability to work independently and represent our brand with integrity.

Benefits:
- Exclusive representation rights for our company in your country.
- Competitive commission-based compensation.
- Access to high-quality products/services with a strong market presence.
- Ongoing support and training from our dedicated team.
- Participation in our yearly meetings in Canada, the USA, and elsewhere.

If you meet the criteria and are ready to seize this exciting opportunity, contact us today with your resume and a brief introduction highlighting your qualifications. Join us in driving our Canadian company to new heights!

Email: Rep@ISCASC.com
Website: www.ISCASC.com

INTERNATIONAL **STANDARD** CERTIFICATION

MALAYSIA

ARMENIA

Our office in Toronto will be opening soon.

WWW.ISCASC.COM – SPRING 2024

We look forward to hearing from you

www.ISCASC.com
contact@ISCASC.com
1-877-307-3077

Vancouver, BC CANADA

www.ingramcontent.com/pod-product-compliance
Lightning Source LLC
Chambersburg PA
CBHW040223040426
42333CB00051B/3424